Living with Serious Mental Illness and Physical Disabilities

by

Jonathan Harnisch

Harnisch Productions LLC

In Association with Babydude Press LLC

36 Mariquita Lane

Corrales, New Mexico 87048

United States of America

Jonathan Harnisch

While the publishers and the author have taken every care in preparing the material included in this work, any statements made as to the legal or other implications of any transaction, any particular method of litigation, or any kind of compensation claim are made in good faith purely for general guidance and cannot be regarded as a substitute for professional advice. Consequently, no liability can be accepted for loss or expense incurred as a result of relying on particular circumstances on statements made in this work.

© Jonathan Harnisch 2016.

All rights reserved. No part of this publication may be reproduced, stored in a retrieval system, or transmitted in any way or by any means, including photocopying or recording, without the written permission of the copyright holder, application for which should be addressed to the publisher.

Crown Copyright material is reproduced with kind permission of the Controller of Her Majesty's Stationery Office.

ISBN-13: 978-1523445479

ISBN-10: 1523445475

Printed in the United States of America and the United Kingdom

First Edition

Good morning everyone. Hello to all my friends around the world! Have a magnificent day! Just do your best in all you do, even if you fall short!

No matter how you feel, get up, dress up, show up, and never give up.

Whenever I can, through all the good and bad times, through thick and thin, I want to inspire people. I want someone to look at me or think of me and say: "Because of you, I did not give up... I don't give up!"

If your big dream scares the shit out of you, you're really onto something. In fact, that's your crystal ball answering the question of "should I do this?" Live a kick-ass life. You deserve it!

Living with schizophrenia and therefore with a brain that from time to time doesn't work, my life can be difficult, but I keep moving ahead, as always, knowing I am a good person and that I am worth it.

Just breathe... In every moment we begin again.

Considering that I have been diagnosed with schizophrenia, bipolar disorder, PTSD, borderline personality disorder, Tourette's syndrome, diabetes, anxiety and depression, a rare blood disease, dyslexia, and cancer, I am doing okay. At the end of the storm, there's always a golden sky.

We have to fight the bad days to earn the best days of our lives.

If you or a loved one has schizophrenia, do not let it possess you. Fight your fucking hardest. Give it your all, and do everything you can to fight the war with your own mind. Never ever give up doing your damnedest to live the life that you want to live, no matter what. Do not ever fucking give up, no matter what your mental health diagnosis is or even if you are just dealing with the fucked up mess of life. In the meantime, if you are having a good day you had better fucking appreciate it because these are extremely rare for people like me diagnosed with a severe mental and terminal physical illness.

Love me or hate me. That's up to you. Believe in yourself, and always keep hope and faith alive—no matter what!

Never give up! Keep on fighting. Don't let your demons beat you.

I will have been 13-years drug- and alcohol-free on Friday. On Saturday I will have been off cigarettes for one month (30 days). My 40th birthday is on Sunday.

My apologies for bringing up something so uninspiring, but I have to vent for a second. One of my bank accounts and my PayPal accounts were compromised three days ago. I have no help. I don't want help, as feeling ignored by everyone in my real and personal life can be a scapegoat. I have done everything I can. I have lost $6,000 so far. This has brought up severe PTSD symptoms. I feel stuck. It is complicated because the account isn't under my name. As with everything with me and my mental illnesses, "it's complicated"—as my doctor proclaims. Where is my wife? My life? My mind? Schizophrenic. Where is my family? For crying out loud! And so I have locked myself in my office again for the day, cancelling all appointments. I don't like days like this. But they pass.

Welcome, everybody, to Wonderland — effing Wonderland. I am feeling a bit better and stronger now. The below is some writing therapy I did earlier today, unedited. I feel so indebted to you all, even those who have left me for example on my Facebook page. Many of you have written suggesting that I am exhausted and in need of rest, relaxation, and some time off. I plan to do so, but we will see whether or not I succeed in taking time off to face the universe literally and devastatingly alone.

Lately, I look into the mirror every day and see a sleepless and lost stranger in myself, as well as in others in my "real" interpersonal and conventionally accepted life. I have been battling severe comorbid schizophrenia and related psychotic and dissociative mental health conditions for most of my life now as well as other "normal" life issues. I feel that it might be time for me to submit — perhaps surrender — and allow my mental and physical health conditions to take over my life experiences, permitting me to live a great deal more — if not fully — in the delusional and hallucinatory landscape of the world where I am most familiar and comfortable. Thank you for understanding, if you do.

Overall, I am exhausted and need some time off. Thank you, everybody. I feel much better having written out these feelings, feeling otherwise abandoned, neglected, abused, controlled, cornered, trapped, and stuck. I need time to think and work on some art projects. I want to become cut off from the world. I just want to be alone for a while. This morning I had an important medical appointment for some blood conditions I have endured over the last couple of years. I am still surviving. I would rather not go into detail about it. It's just scary. I am trying to hold onto the saying that most things we worry about don't happen. I've done all I can since the last visit to the doctor's for this problem. I'll just say that it is potentially life threatening. But... I will end it there.

It's just a little scary, so I am now cutting up some random old film stock here in my production office to bring back memories from when I began shooting film on Super 8; I have also been watching some early video, documenting my life. It feels nostalgic to see some of the footage after 20 or 30 years. Sometimes I miss certain aspects of times past. But I'll be around. I am just so happy. I went on my own for the first time, as I am usually overwhelmed by all the people and lights, to the Apple Store to finally get my main computer fixed after months and months of using an iPhone as my desktop.

It's a strange experience to know that I probably have five years or so left to live. It makes you think and cry. But I look at the world in a whole different way—just in case, you know? But I am not upset about it. I don't quite know why.

I invited my father out to visit the other day. We've been estranged since 2010. I am also giving away some of my expensive gadgets and other objects, like my top-of-the-line 3D TV, to some of the staff here on my compound. I don't need these things. I like them, but I've worked hard this year and actually made enough money on my own: not so much from book sales and film and TV checks from my film distributor but mostly from Wall Street, my primary career, as I am technically a hedge fund manager, like my father, just on a smaller scale, of course.

I don't know. I feel as if all I am doing is making up things to get sympathy. I do not like that about myself, not one bit. Sometimes you have to be your own hero. Schizophrenia is a devastating illness that affects approximately 1% of the population. Its primary impact is on thought, and its cardinal symptom is psychotic thinking in the individuals that it affects. It can also affect many aspects of our cortical function. Although great strides have occurred in treating this disorder, it remains one of the most debilitating psychiatric disorders. And here I am, living with a terminal illness and diagnosed with something new every year—for the past 40 years. I was a stillborn. I feel like Stephen Hawking, smile, emoticon, surviving schizophrenia, bipolar disorder, PTSD, borderline personality disorder, Tourette's syndrome, diabetes, anxiety and depression, a rare blood disease, dyslexia, and cancer…. I will soon be having an MRI for a cyst in the pituitary gland in my brain.

I am a survivor. I am my own hero. I have lived this long with achievements and failures, all the while in an overarching cognitive decline. Losing your mind, with schizophrenia, is difficult, but, I must admit, losing your awareness makes you wiser. If you know somebody with similar problems, please pick up the phone and call him or her, or send a text message. Just see how they are without any expectations or attempts to fix them. Trust me, it might make a difference. It might not seem so, but it really might make a huge difference. I speak from experience.

I wish I could write more, but my fingers are cramped from the side effects of all the antipsychotic medication. It began in 1988. It was 12. 80mg of Haldol. My life has changed ever since. This is life. This is my life. Right now. It's my perspective. The only perspective I know, real or unreal. The six knock-out vitamins, two per hour, helped me sleep longer, despite a blood condition that is affected by excess of liquids. And then the diabetes insipidus. And so on. I am just doing what I want to do. I mean, I can't even have more than a glass of water a day or else I will end up back again in the emergency room. It's a silly disease. Real, yes, but worth a diet of basically no liquids? No. Not now. One thing at a time, and my fingers and limbs are so tense and cramped from the Thorazine I am on; it is hard, but I always, always come through into the light.

My own work is helping me as well. I have been sipping the liquids since 6:30 a.m., and I am having some trouble sequencing my thoughts; I am putting a hold on my next novel so that I can shy away from avant-garde heavy duty and difficult reading… Blah, Blip, Bam, and Boom! Can I kick it? Yes, sure I can. I am kicking butt. As for PayPal and Wells Fargo, I have decided to close the account at WF today, at the branch, just down the street. I'll walk. It's fine. No one is here—again—to help. Jonathan and the "billionaire schizophrenic" bull. Sociopaths run my life. That is my perspective, my point of view. It is real to me. I don't need paychecks from Peconic Partners, my father's firm, nor from my art or my bestselling books. My father controls my other trust accounts in any case. I don't know. Blah…

The cognitive decline is not funny, and seeing my father in January? Another misunderstanding. Now he has said he is NOT coming out BECAUSE I asked him not to when I said DO come out. That is schizophrenia! I feel estranged from my wife. But since I began this, I have been feeling better and stronger. Maybe I will take a shower soon. I am trying to drain my Wells Fargo account so that the PayPal hacker will not be able to pay for things with it. I own quite a bit of PayPal stock on Wall

Street. I am selling all of it today. I laugh at my love for the company and my investment in its common stock, but I've never trusted PayPal nor eBay, and I have never used either in my life.

Success in life comes when you refuse to give up — with goals so strong that obstacles, failure, and loss only act as motivation.

A depressed person may experience feelings of sadness. I had a lot to give to this world especially when I was feeling great, and I always hoped and prayed that one morning I would wake up, and all the distress would be over, but it was too hard for too long. I couldn't do it. And so, I am sad to report — I have slept on this several times — I have given up at last. I have lost all hope.

I am terrified of my early onset schizophrenia — a serious chronic mental illness that causes delusional and hallucinogenic thoughts. The primary symptom of the rare blood disease with which I was diagnosed in December 2015 (I can never remember the name) is the same as the symptom mentioned above for schizophrenia. I feel as if I am losing my mind. It is terrifying. My negative behavioral and thinking processes, as well as my confusion, have been elevated beyond belief. I just can't think straight for the life of me. I have been sleeping fine, my diet is OK, and I am taking my medication as prescribed. I believe my doctors, family, and caregivers are plotting to institutionalize me.

If any of you experience the same, please know you are not the only one. I celebrate 13 years clean and sober later this week. Nausea, dizziness, memory problems, confusion, and more. MRI soon for the brain tumor. I just want to live. I just want to live! Have a good evening. I will catch up with your hundreds of comments another time. I hope you can forgive me for being behind. I am trying to juggle too many balls at once, and I just can't think straight or remember anything. My entire medical team is on high alert, so I do have help and support no matter where my thinking goes regarding posting online in the future—as I am paranoid concerning those who are here to help. They apparently really are here to help! This is the greatest battle I have ever fought. Worse than quitting even the worst "junk" years and year ago. My life has not turned out how I thought it would. I am completely trapped.

My mood changes. Mozart's music—his noted Serenade in B-flat, K. 361, "Gran partita": III Adagio. Thank you. And welcome, new followers. You happened to catch me at an awkward time, on a bit of a detour if you will. I don't know. My cognitive abilities are declining, seemingly by the minute. My experiences have become so frightening that I can't even begin to tell you about them; I just want to live and be free of all of this. But I am not out of the woods yet.

Sometimes I can't believe how much I have accomplished in my life—just by getting by every day with my severe health limitations. I'm beginning to see the light, ceasing to care anymore whom I please or what anyone says about me. Therefore, I can now produce the best work I am capable of: living with terminal illness. My specialty care doctor said something to the effect of, "Jonathan, it is a wonder how you have ever done a thing much less get up and be alive, literally, for the past 20 years or so, when all this started." I provided her with the medical records I dug up, proving that I have had a rare terminal illness since I was born. To be more precise, I was born with this. I was a stillborn—three days with no natural breath and no natural heartbeat—just a life support system maintaining any possible life inside me. And 40 years later, I hope (I turn 40 in less than a week.), I am still here. I happened to survive.

Tuesday, December 15, 2015, 5:00 a.m. Email update. Dr. K. (cognitive behavioral psychologist), Dr. F. (medical doctor, schizophrenia), and M. (wife): See you at noon (or so)! We're on! :) Note: Physical health is becoming of concern. My wife has explained this better than me. Plus, to be honest, it is personally terrifying. I want you to know that. (Compassion appreciated, gentleness, etc., "bedside manner," if you will). But I am doing all I can and succeeding so far. Not too much is set in stone yet (ongoing). As far as I see, though my work with diabetes did improve the A1C. Will see a dermatologist for yet another new hopefully benign growth on back; blood (sodium levels) drastically in decline causing a great deal, if not most, of my cognitive decline over the years. Barely any memory left, lost, confused, and so forth. M. can fill you in w/ detail (might be a good idea), but I hope we can once again focus session today on the task at hand. Please keep in mind cognition is dramatically worse even since Thursday; we're taking care of it. It is scary, but it feels a bit like Alzheimer's (it is not—I just mean the symptoms/cognition). I might not be able to track you at all in the session; additional medications will likely improve thirst and the urine matter rather quickly, within days. Physical (sodium/blood) possibility of diabetes insipidus (and there are two kinds of diabetes insipidus, apparently, still learning). Saw specialty doctor yesterday and will have another fasting blood test early this morning for additional screenings, which may not return results for quite a bit longer than most common tests. I can interpret the visit to the doctor yesterday — with my wife. I was proactive — also with other life things like going out (on my own), taking care of things that I have not been able to do during the past few years, but still, of course, not driving myself. Back to blood levels, today and upcoming, in addition to my request for cancer screening, specifically a white blood cell test of some kind — which apparently seems fine according to the current results, but there are more to come and therefore it is a threat. But I have not been scared.

"Lost," with thoughts and memories right in front of me. I just can't reach them. That is how it all feels. I believe my lungs and heart give cause for concern — my cigarette smoking drastically increased to four or five packs daily for a while. Stress — again terrifying. Maintaining as much resilience as I can through the terror. One thing at a time.

There is, as you might see, a lot going on, medically: medication, medication additions, and probably changes—trial and error stuff. More changes to occur until we figure out what is going on. My art is what keeps me as well as I am, with my mood fluxes, and I am successfully back on Latuda. Day three, now without nausea, with or without food, go figure! All we know—to communicate it most simply—is that something physical is causing the rapid mental decline. The worst case, of course, is ICU, but all is sufficiently OK, for now, and I am getting the medical assistance I need. Just to mention—as cancer gets compassion and "acceptance"—it is good to know that physical issues can cause a large number of mental issues. It reassures me. Please be as gentle as you are by nature.

Even if I didn't complete a thought above, the immediate point is that I will be ready to see you at noon. I'll be here! Thanks!

"Miracles in the Heart of Darkness" by Jonathan Harnisch

September 6, 2012, Porcelain Utopia

There are times in life when I have to deal with "awful" things; things I just can't ignore. The way I cope is to give such things all the time and attention they need — but not one single second longer than that. I invite you to do the same.

Take the time to enjoy all the good and beauty life has to offer.

As I have often mentioned on The Real Me podcast, Porcelain Utopia, and my documentaries, throughout the years of my own darkness (and even light) — all of it, especially the loss of my family, finances, and my mind (and even the loss of over 1,000 hours of film and video footage I had shot since I was 11) — I always had hope. At one time (I think it's in one of my other documentaries) I speak candidly, in my own self-aware psychosis, about having nothing, at least nothing "good," and that I didn't even want help. But even then I always had hope. It started with my not knowing what I was even hoping for (perhaps a miracle, or just some relief—wanting to press the pause button of life); from there came patience, then mindfulness, and then the camera, which I'd look into, just talking to my then-invisible audience. Spirituality was always there, and, even with the schizophrenia, I had my "imaginary friends" (if that makes sense). The "positive" symptoms (voices and hallucinations)—both good and evil (the "good," the angels, always cancelled out the "evil")—told me I was brilliant and gave me brilliant ideas, mostly of a grandiose nature, but then again most of my life has been rather grand and abundant.

Certain well-respected theorists (Carl Jung, John Weir Perry, and R.D. Laing) take the approach that there is so much we don't know about life, but science might even suggest that such symptoms could very well be real in some way, including all the loss and trauma, for example, and the idea, not even a belief necessarily, that "everything happens for a reason..." I still couldn't see the meaning, so I came up with my own, and then hope became my purpose. It grew, changed, and evolved, as did my authenticity and lately my self-acceptance and forgiveness of others' actions, especially my own, as well as the way that I look at the world.

I took the leap, and when I began to change the way I thought (which can be difficult with schizophrenia), my values changed—also out of need—and, with time, the miracles started to occur—just not as I had expected. Sometimes I simply have to stay put and let go completely. It's often impossible for me not to get caught up in the moment of negativity, whether I have just bruised my hand on a door or some drawn-out legal matter is haunting every minute of the day. But once I get that far and start simultaneously thinking about, believing, and feeling all the clichéd quotes that I have sometimes posted on Porcelain Utopia and elsewhere, I see that they're all incredibly true. Currently, I've been choosing which things in my life I want to deal with, deciding to do one thing at a time in my own way. Being true to myself first, then others, and, when I miss the mark, I start over.

If any of you are still struggling (I think that we are all in need of healing in some way or another), I'm confident you will succeed and come out of the darkness which, as most of you already know, is where the light is.

I'm so happy that I have touched so many of you in some way. My goal has always been to affect just one person, but now my "audience" is well over 100 million. To some I'm just some mental health problem; to my best friends and myself, I am a person. As we all are. What we have in common is Love. I could write volumes about this, and actually I do have many movies, books, and works of art—not online, just on my list. But most are complete.

As I wrote to a close friend this morning, "Feel my big bear hug. I feel yours. It's unbelievable."

I received an email from Bill Clinton's office a short while ago [revision: two days ago, having written this part on September 4th] asking me for additional information in order to recognize my work in mental health advocacy. A minute later, the head of a major Hollywood studio I was acquainted with during my years working in Los Angeles and New York wrote me about a $200 million period piece film script I'd written that's been sitting on my shelf for over ten years, as well as on his shelf. They are apparently going to green light the film after all this time.

My browser, the Internet, and even my website crashed for a minute, and the two emails and all the data have been instantly deleted. I am an official developer for Google (I use Gmail and Chrome) and have owned Google stock since day one—worth over $1.2 billion today. My family took control of this in January 2010. I have no credit and no money; my credit score had been around 780–790, and now I'm still in debt.

The finances that allowed me to purchase Google IPO came from a conceptual patent which, as I have written and spoken of in the past, outlined the initial online shopping interface for Price Club. It was called the Price Club Quest. It still exists as a kiosk in most major retail stores today. My father was a founding financier of the company at the time (1991 — I was 15, and the Internet had just been released to the public by the British). Companies such as Amazon, Wal-Mart, and Target have benefited from my idea. I have held onto the original dated and signed records.

Today [again, two days ago now], it was confirmed by a notable patent attorney contact who wrote me an hour or two after I wrote him that I do indeed have all I need, even without an actual patent, to avoid court; to get the patent itself, the records are all that is needed. I scanned him a copy, chiefly a forty-page piece of writing with diagrams, research, analysis, and the like.

[Still, 2 days ago...] I'm deciding on a sort of vow of poverty in this matter. Within, I assume, a few months — I don't know — and with no fee, I could quadruple my actual net worth which was removed from me because I am mentally ill — perhaps brilliantly "insane" (ugh...). However, I have chosen not to pursue this, even though it would simply be a matter of replying, "Yes, I'll hand over the Price Club Quest file." He would even come out here to avoid any errors or loss of mail via the carrier.

I want my life, and I have it today. I receive perhaps the greatest gifts via email — miracles. All I want to do is spend time on my farm — with our horses, goats, donkeys, ducks, dogs, cats, and birds. All I want to do is make my music therapy tunes and my homemade iMovie and YouTube videos, as well as help one of my best friends in the world who happens to have once been the most famous person in the world. He now struggles himself.

I have now stabilized for over three months on my medication and therapy regimen for my diagnosis with a rare schizophrenia spectrum disorder with autistic features that often presents me with gifts, "visions," and miracles. My otherwise bad day does not mean I have a bad life. Right now, in the heat of my own darkness and in my dilemma, which is in my favor, I just want to continue what I am doing and so decline credit or restitution, instead simply helping people feel okay with their own mental health issues by offering inspiration when I am able to. It is enough just to know of my countless achievements in film and TV which have entertained millions and which others in the world—and myself—can purchase on the Internet. I think my job is done.

This might very well be my last actual blog post on Porcelain Utopia [note: currently defunct] and my last recording on the old The Real Me Podcast [note: currently defunct]. Things change, and we'll just have to see. I'm just longing for a simpler life, eliminating stress and the pressure I feel to constantly produce and create. This often becomes too much for me: to feel the need and, for the most part, to do. At any rate, I am approaching my work as something much less imperative, so I can focus more on my own health and life, making choices and decisions which sometimes change.

I've already sent in my letters of resignation for my work developing software for Google, Apple, and Microsoft. I have saved all my royalty checks from my published anthologies, as the physical checks framed on my wall mean more than $50 here or $100 there.

I know who I am, and I know what I want. I know that I change. We all change, and we survive. We get through it.

I have made my mark on the world in all areas of my craft, and they've been confirmed. I helped others. I "did good," as we New Yorkers say.

Happy travels on your own path. May you be blessed enough to find and follow your dreams, not anybody else's. Trust me, it will make you happier, perhaps enlightened.

Thank you for being such a wonderful, supportive, and considerate audience all this time — I might post now and then in the future, and Porcelain Utopia will be up until 2015 as funding is limited. Other than that, I don't believe much more can or even should be said. I have reached all my goals today, ironically all at once. I can live with that, and I can go and watch some TV and listen to some Duran Duran albums, as I do every day to help keep me going — to stay afloat.

[Now… this evening, two days later on 06 September, 2012, 7:30 p.m., as I wait for a project to export, here is a brief update, as I was not planning to have published the above. But now, regarding those miracles…]

7:20 p.m.: Speak of the Devil. Having written the above in order to write for therapy, it turns out this morning that I have sold a new film and TV program. Wow! I suppose things work out in the end. I had begun writing this a day or two earlier, and now my new medicine regimen has in fact kicked in, and my networks in Hollywood and in the literary world are actually coming through, with over 200 emails and messages every hour now. This is apparently due to all the effort I've been putting in over the past few years. It's paying off now, by the hour. I believe this is only the beginning. I am coming back. No, I am back. And I have got it!

Coming on 7:30 p.m. I think it's about time to actually post this. It began on Tuesday, and things can really change in a day or two. I will keep you posted on the show and will keep on with the rebuilding of broken links here on this site, adding more posts when I get that miracle of just a little bit of time. Perhaps a real God does exist. I always had that hope. And to get back to my professional life, it is looking to be on the up and up. I must say, I am proud of myself. I am forgiving and grateful and feel peace of mind again—at last.

I sure love to write. But off I go now to develop my upcoming motion picture and its musical score—an oblique and surreal feature length film called *Prototype*. It's one of those passion projects of mine. It looks like the money will be coming in after all thanks to my television sales. Relief. The contract is simple and being revised slightly overnight. It will be in and done by tomorrow, Friday. At the latest by early next week. Can't wait to let you know about it further. I am simply not at leisure to do so at the moment. But it's real and happening. It's amazing. I want to keep this one safe, friends, and not "jinx" it. And Bill Clinton, well, maybe his office will write back at some point. If not, nothing lost and everything already gained, in my opinion.

Again, please take the time to enjoy all the good and beauty life has to offer; it's sublime when you are able to see it that way— when you can see this realistically.

Since the closing down of Porcelain Utopia in October 2013, Jonathan Harnisch has decrypted as much code and text as possible, which thousands of hackers had corrupted, breaking through the most sophisticated security software available. The former self-hosted WordPress website, narrating Harnisch's journey through schizophrenia, wielded Harnisch 25 million hits per day by its end and was described in the press as the most viral WordPress blog that is known of. This is what remains.

Here's the gist of what my cognitive behavioral therapy psychologist and I discussed during today's appointment.

Notes from my doctor:

I noticed how much more at ease you appeared after things seemed copacetic with everyone. You stated, "Well, things are not ok, but my attitude is ok." That really got me thinking about the power of our perceptions—and the impact they can have. I then thought we should discuss the pros and cons of chaos vs. calm. I understand you have some strong feelings about chaos and calm—and I thought a practical analysis of this would be beneficial.

This all then led me to think, "Jonathan has a pretty nice set-up. If we could figure out a way for him to sit back and accept more things—maybe he'd be happier and more at peace overall!" Again, I bring all this up b/c you end up suffering more than anyone when things become overwhelming.

I brought up the idea that the "forest"—the big picture— is one in which your father set up a trust. As far as I understand it, the trust is intended to support you with a very decent lifestyle for as long as you live. That includes the property, all your necessities, and all the money you get biweekly and for the holidays.

I think you have ended up hyper-vigilant about the "trees"—the details—because you believe you should be getting more than what's being provided to you. From what you've described, this goes back to not getting financial recognition for your ideas, not being provided with nearly as much money as you believe you are worth, and not having as much freedom as you'd like to do what you want with your money. I also believe your traumatic experiences have a lot to do with this and the fact that people have taken advantage of you in the past.

In addition, I think there are real things that occur daily that may be frustrating. So, when you identify a "tree" that bothers you, I think there's often some truth to it! I do not think many of these things are delusional! But rather they are the type of cognitive distortion that all human beings deal with.

So, what does this all mean? Well, I guess it all comes down to strategy. It reminded me of that gamble in which you can take a high-risk (e.g., 1/100) chance of getting 1 billion dollars or nothing OR a no-risk guarantee of receiving 10 million dollars. I feel that all the frustration and anger you feel, and the resultant behaviors, have essentially led you in the direction of taking the high-risk chance — instead of just accepting the 10 million.

I understand this may not seem fair, and I am certainly not one to suggest someone just settle for less. But I feel as if the focus on the trees ends up upsetting you over and over again — and then everyone else around you. And the ultimate consequences of only focusing on the trees could be a lot worse than the guaranteed no-risk "compromise." The fact is — we are all really trying to set things up so you can indefinitely live on the compound and enjoy life as much as possible. But-there could be a point in which we can't sustain what you may need. When you focus on the trees, it exacerbates this. I've discussed my limitations with respect to being a sole practitioner with a full practice. And your wife is tasked with managing quite a lot. We want to help—but we cannot provide an infinite source of support.

I likened the whole thing to accepting that you'll never be able to purchase a Ferrari and have to "settle" instead for a top-of-the-line BMW. (And you pointed out: at least it wasn't a Honda Civic.) It's not ideal—but swinging for the fences may just not be practical all the time.

I really believe we would all rather have you feel healthy and be thinking clearly and handling your own resources. But, because of the circumstances, we are tasked with being the board members for you in your role as CEO. We are happy to do it—for as long as we can. But let's try to focus on the forest—and not the trees!

Wednesday, December 16, 2015, Update: 6:26 a.m. I just received some additional news regarding my health. Indeed, it's been confirmed: I do have diabetes insipidus. Outward Bound! Text from my wife: "Honey, I'm sorry you worried so much. What I wanted to tell you is that the pharmacy called; [the doctor] ordered desmopressin, the medication for diabetes insipidus (DI), which indicates that you have that. However, the pharmacy is out of desmopressin (DI is not a common disorder), and it won't be in until Monday. I will call [the doctor] later today and see where we go from here."

I have been keeping some health conditions (and possible health conditions) to myself since my hospital visit last month when I almost lost my life. I might have to get an MRI due to my rare blood condition; this, aside from my complex mental health conditions—primarily those within the schizophrenia spectrum syndrome—is likely caused by complex trauma. But I have reason to live. As for the possible cyst in my pituitary gland and losing vision, I'll write about some of the "consider me a rare case" material I have been gathering since December. Currently, nobody medical is immediately concerned, so things look okay enough for now. I have just been getting blood tests and making consistent and continuous visits to the hospital and endocrinologist.

My apologies, for I can barely type through nausea and lack of control over my fingers. I'll see if I can drop this text into one of the editing programs I use to write my literature. Before reading what is below, please know that my latest blood test, which tested for quite a number of possibilities that are complicated by the antipsychotic medication I am on, will likely show that the cyst is benign; but if it is not, it can apparently be treated with medication. Pituitary tumors (adenomas) that do not secrete active hormones are known as clinically nonfunctioning pituitary adenomas. Most are large (macroadenomas), measuring more than one centimeter in size at the time of diagnosis. Patients start experiencing symptoms when the giant tumor compresses the optic nerves, leading to vision loss or the loss of normal pituitary function. Clinically, nonfunctioning pituitary adenomas make up about half of pituitary adenomas. The vast majority of these are benign.

There are several possible reasons why nonfunctioning pituitary adenomas can occur. Typically, the body produces hormones by taking a larger molecule and cutting it at the right places to create a functioning hormone. In some cases, something is wrong with this cutting process, and a "functional" hormone fails to be produced. The hormone might still travel into the bloodstream, but it is inactive and usually cannot be detected by using standard blood tests. In some cases, the hormone might be formed inside the cell, but there is something wrong with the transport process that is required to release it into the bloodstream. In other cases, the tumor cells do not produce a hormone. The most common symptoms are due to the large tumor compressing nearby structures, leading to vision loss or bitemporal hemianopsia. When large pituitary adenomas (macroadenomas) grow upward into the brain cavity, the tumor can elevate and compress the optic chiasm. A loss of the outer peripheral vision is called bitemporal hemianopsia. When severe, patients can only see what is directly in front of them; many patients do not become aware of their visual loss until it is quite difficult. Other obvious problems include loss of visual acuity (blurry vision), especially if the macroadenoma grows forward and compresses an optic nerve, and inability to recognize colors as brightly as usual.

I just want to live to be 40 on January 17th, 2016. I have hope.

SOMEONE IN YOUR LIFE NEEDS TO HEAR THAT THEY MATTER. They are loved. They have a future. You can tell them. This could be you. This could be me—somebody struggling with a mental health condition. Please reach out today, no matter the outcome. Just send a text, give them a call, and write them a note by email. You get what I'm saying, right? Just for today, if you would, I invite you just to say hello and ask

about them. Have a conversation if you can. No expectations —
just the tiniest random act of kindness. It will make a difference.
You may not be able to fix them. Just give it a shot if you will. It
would mean a lot to me, personally, if you did. I'm home now
from the hospital, and I must say it's quite a readjustment, even
after just three days away in the intensive care unit. Thank you
for all your supportive comments. This page is meant for some,
not all. The door is always open to come or go. I just do what I
do, of course, sometimes knowing that I do not necessarily
practice what I preach. And there is that whole thing that many
of you call being honest — and therefore inspiring. I do not agree.
I am not honest. Nor inspiring. All of my work, and I mean all,
is for me. This stuff helps me. Of course, I am glad it helps you
sometimes. I just need to do this, whether it's a post saying
"Dear Life, you suck" or "today is a good day to have a great
day."

I don't know what I am doing. I don't think anyone does. OK,
here's what I am saying just as it comes into my head — it's like a

road trip. You plan it out, use a map, and stay on course. You have fun. Students! A detour comes. You get off track and lose your sense of direction. Are you with me? It might not be coming out the right way, but I think you follow me. So, on this hypothetical road trip, you get lost, essentially, and the trip turns into a whole new unplanned experience in a wild new way. It ends. You're back home. And it's over. All that's left are the memories. I could go on and on. Just stay strong guys. We are ALL fighting some battle. Again, I could go on and on, really, but I won't. I won't. Not right now. Maybe in 10 minutes. I just don't know. That might be the whole message in this little early morning writing session. By the way, this is the fourth day without a cigarette—just a set of electronic cigarettes. Extremely limited liquid intake. Caffeine. Time to chill out a bit, if I can. Of course, no need to apologize, but forgive my typos and my unedited writing—these pet peeves that I have. Life's tough. But it's OK. Thanks.

Life is hard. Healing hurts. Moving forward is terrifying for many people.

Have a good day. You are amazing. Remember that. If you have the power to make someone happy, please do it. The world needs more of that.

—Jonathan Harnisch

Facebook: www.facebook.com/jwharnisch

www.ingramcontent.com/pod-product-compliance
Lightning Source LLC
Chambersburg PA
CBHW071302280526
45788CB00004B/1812